MW00332577

FAT MOONS
AND
HUNGER MOONS

This is a companion book to *Whispers of the Ancients: Native Tales for Teaching and Healing in Our Time*—co-authored with Moses (Amik) Beaver.

© MOSES AMIK BEAVER S.L.BJ 04

FAT MOONS AND HUNGER MOONS

The Turn of the Seasons for Northwoods Natives

TAMARACK SONG & MOSES (AMIK) BEAVER

SNOW WOLF PUBLISHING

SNOW WOLF PUBLISHING

7124 Military Road, Three Lakes, Wisconsin 54562
www.snowwolfpublishing.org

Snow Wolf Publishing is a division of Teaching Drum Outdoor School
Copyright © 2021 by Tamarack Song and Moses Amik Beaver

All rights reserved. No part of this book may be reproduced or utilized in any form or by any means, electronic or mechanical, including photocopying, recording, or by any information storage and retrieval system, without first obtaining written permission from the publisher.

Song, Tamarack, 1948—Fat Moons and Hunger Moons: The Turn of the Seasons for Northwoods Natives

ISBN: 978-0-9966561-0-8

Cover, text design, and layout by Sherry Roberts of The Roberts Group— www.editorialservice.com

Cover artwork by Moses Amik Beaver

To send correspondence, mail a first class letter to Tamarack Song, c/o Snow Wolf Publishing, 7124 Military Road, Three Lakes, Wisconsin 54562; or email Tamarack at info@snowwolfpublishing.org.

Visit Tamarack's websites at www.healingnaturecenter.org, www.teachingdrum.org, and www.snowwolfpublishing.org.

References to Internet websites (URLs) were accurate at the time of writing. Neither the authors nor Snow Wolf Publishing are responsible for URLs that may have expired or changed since this book was published.

All proceeds from the sale of this book go to nonprofits dedicated to environmental restoration and the continuation of indigenous cultures.

CONTENTS

DEDICATION

MOSES (AMIK) BEAVER: 1960–2017

Moses Amik S.L.B. '02

"WINDIGO, WINDIGO, PLEASE don't steal my soul!"—a line from an old Ojibwe story that haunted Moses (Amik) Beaver, my dear friend from the *Nibinamik** (Summer Beaver) Ojibwe Reserve in Northern Ontario. Moses illustrated the story for the collection of traditional legends titled *Whispers of the Ancients*, which we co-authored in 2010. *Night of the Windigo* was the last tale in the book. Its telling not only inspired his most soul-gripping artwork, but it also served as a disquieting reminder for the trajectory of his life.

Windigos are walking dead. They are the shells of people who were banished from their villages for some heinous offense. Having no reason to live or die, they wander aimlessly in the wilderness. Sometimes they lurk in the shadows not far from their old village, in hopes of catching at least a glimpse of a former loved one. Only they never let themselves be seen, as their horrendous appearance could cause someone to drop dead on the spot.

When Moses was a young man, he left Summer Beaver—a remote community with the weekly mail plane as the only outside contact. This kept the Reserve an oasis of traditional Ojibwe culture, with close-knit clan, a subsistence-based lifestyle, and Ojibwe as the first language.

That all changed in Thunder Bay—the big city in North Ontario where many young people who leave the isolated Reserves end

---

* All Native words are in the Ojibwe dialect of the Algonquian language, which is spoken in the band of Northcountry stretching from North Dakota through the Great Lakes and northward to Hudson Bay, then eastward to New England and the Maritime provinces. For simplicity's sake, most Ojibwe words are presented in their singular form, and they are italicized when first introduced.

up. With the endless stream of low-grade food and the loneliness brought on by a crowded city of strangers, Moses soon felt like a walking dead. And the Windigo story became his story.

The day came when Moses decided he had enough of a life without living. He stripped himself of everything that identified him as something other than himself. Before the day ended, he was in jail, where he was found expired on the cold concrete floor of his cell on February 13, 2017.

To add pain to misery, Moses's elder sister, Mary Wabasse, died in a car accident on the way down to Thunder Bay to tend to what remained of her "little-big" brother.

Moses and I called each other "brother," in part because we both knew the pangs of banishment, and we both struggled to scratch our ways back to the realm of the living. We talked many times about what it was like to lurk in the shadows and peer from the outside, in. It drew us together.

The only words I had to send with him on his Journey to the Spirit World were "Eat fresh!"

Whenever we called each other, it was "Eat fresh!" instead of "Hello." And whenever we parted, it was "Eat fresh!" instead of "Good-bye."

It all started when he and I were driving down to my place late one night from Sault Ste. Marie, Ontario, where I picked him up from the airport. It was ten o'clock, we were still a few hours from home, and we were hungry. For miles, all the eateries we passed were closed.

Then, seemingly out of the blue, Moses shouted, "Eat fresh!" Sure enough, there was a neon "Eat fresh!" sign in the window of an open Subway. We stopped for a couple of tuna fish subs, which were soon gone, yet "Eat fresh!" stuck with us.

When I got the call on that fateful day in February 2017, the most meaningful parting words I could come up with were, "Moses, may you now 'Eat fresh!' again, and forever."

I met Moses by way of a newspaper review of an art gallery exhibit. I typically don't read such material, yet the illustration accompanying the review pulled me in. That painting (which you'll

Moses Amik s.l.B 05²

find on page 45) to me embodied the essence of the Old Way.

At the time, I was working on the stories for *Whispers of the Ancients*, and I was looking for an illustrator. I knew right then that I had found him. I called the gallery, and the director put me in touch with Moses's agent.

"I'm sure he'll want to illustrate your book," she replied after I had barely finished describing the project. "You are speaking to the heart of why Moses is an artist. I can't imagine him saying anything other than, 'When can we start?'"

Sure enough, I got a call from Moses and his agent a couple of days later, inviting me to Thunder Bay so we could get to know each other and work out details.

Moses and I resonated immediately, personally and professionally. He would sketch an illustration from my story, and sometimes he would add story details that he remembered from the versions he heard as a Child from the Elders. His finished illustrations would often inspire me to further refine the story.

The result: a university press asked to publish it, readers gave it nothing but top ratings, it was awarded five gold medals, and—most meaningful to both Moses and me—Elders commended us for telling the stories the way they used to be told.

In late 2016, Moses called and said he'd like to collaborate with me on another project. He asked if I might like to do something that conveyed the values and richness of his People's traditional way of life. I replied that I was just about to call him with the same idea. *Fat Moons and Hunger Moons* was born.

With our synergy running high, it felt like the old days again. Yet he soon faded away, and then I got the call.

His former wife Melanie Huddart joined with me to complete *Fat Moons and Hunger Moons*, with artwork of Moses's that was in her possession. We now offer this work as a lasting tribute to the life of a man who—though he trembled under the burden of a crumbling culture—saw his talent as a way to summon the Ancient Ones to come forth and breathe new life into that culture.

Moses, all of us who were gifted with your presence wish you to know that your work continues, just as you and I will never cease to "Eat Fresh!" together.

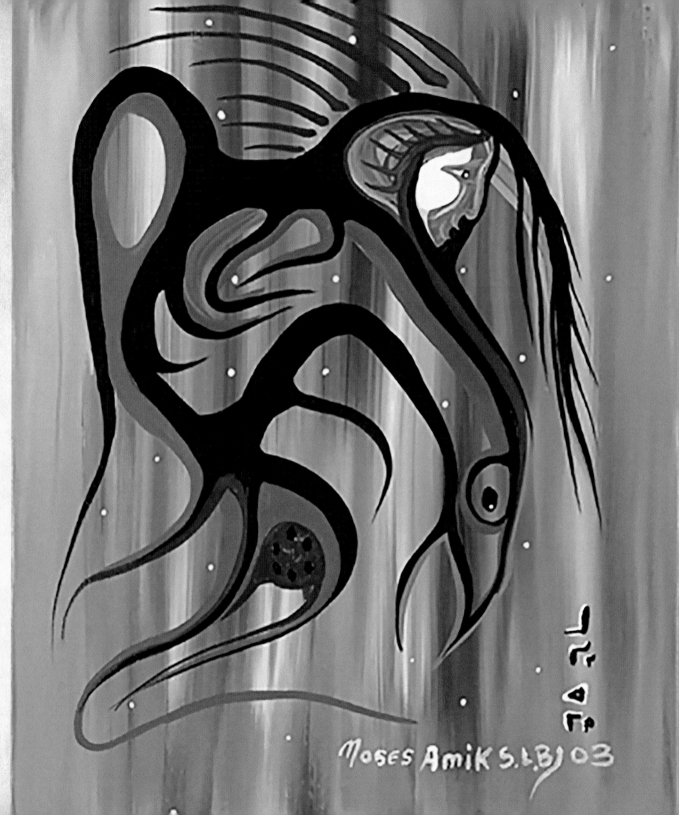

Moses Amik S.L.B.'03

FOREWORD
A RETURN TO THE CIRCLE WAY

MOSES AND I initiated this book project to take us all on a return journey to being fully human. As a people, we have forgotten the stories that once instructed us, we've abandoned the dreams that guided us, and we've turned our backs on the Elders who watched over us. Our Mother Earth has become a distant place we might visit on holiday. We now have more preferred energy sources than Father Sun, and we no longer need Sister Moon to keep track of time.

Those who came together to produce this book along with Moses and me wish it to serve as an inspiration for returning to what we have forgotten, abandoned, and replaced—what many indigenous people call the *Circle Way*. Up until recently for Moses's people, and a little longer ago for non-Native people, everyone lived in the Circle Way. There was no other option than to dwell in Balance with self, each other, and our Mother Planet.

Now, many of us yearn for what we once had. However, what we desire is often placed out of reach, in order that we first become the people needed to maintain it. Returning to the Circle Way stayed too far out of reach for Moses. Yet his spirit lives on through these pages as he inspires us to again become capable of honorably and respectfully Walking the Circle Way.

This is ultimately a healing book. As these pages paint the story of how we all once lived, may we each find sanctuary for our deepest yearnings, along with the resilience to achieve them.

MOONS OF THE NORTHCOUNTRY NATIVES

Moon as Grandmother

For the Native Clanspeople of the Upper Great Lakes region, the Moon is alive. They know her as *Nokomis Giizis* or Grandmother Moon, and they await each time Nokomis grows into her pregnant fullness, when she brings gifts for them, her beloved Grandchildren. Each time Nokomis withers and dies, they know she goes to renew herself so she can return bearing new gifts. Even cold and hunger are gifts that are appreciated and anticipated, for without cold there would be no stories to guide and heal, and without hunger there would be no motivation to forestall starvation.

By consciously living in relationship with Nokomis, the Human People grow in awareness of their relationship with the Winged, Scaled, Furred, and Leafed People. The Humans find they are kin with all—they are all Nokomis's Grandchildren. This is the essence of Balance and the blueprint for living it.

As you walk through the Moons in the coming pages, it would be good to remember that in the Northcountry there are only two seasons: *Niibin*—the Green Season, and *Biboon*—the White Season. What we know as spring and autumn are merely times of tussling between *Giiwedin*, Keeper of the Northern Realm, and *Zhaawan*, Keeper of the Southern Realm. Each of them is passionate about bringing their gifts to the People, yet they cannot both be here at once, so they end up pushing each other back and forth. This is why at the end of each Green Season and White Season, when one grows weak, the other gains advantage and makes an inroad. The weather keeps flip-flopping between cool and warm, wet and dry, until one of them finally tires completely and retreats to his/her realm to rest and replenish.

The Turn of the Seasons

The Green Season is brought on by the warm Winds and rains of Zhaawan, which are pregnant with female energy. Her days are long and lush and her nurturing energy is sensual and kinetic. During the days of Zhaawan, the People are extroverted and drawn to multiple and fast-paced activities and projects.

Long nights, frigid days, and a warm blanket of Snow are the gifts of Giiwedin. His male energy is straightforward, solid, and directed. On the stark, cold nights, his moaning Winds bring the storyline—the ageless, universal source of all stories—raw and close, so the storytellers can give it voice. This is a time of reserved, inward-focused activities.

Living in Balance is living in sync with the seasonal rhythms. They bring times of lushness and times of lean, known as the *Fat Moons* and

Turn of Seasons begins

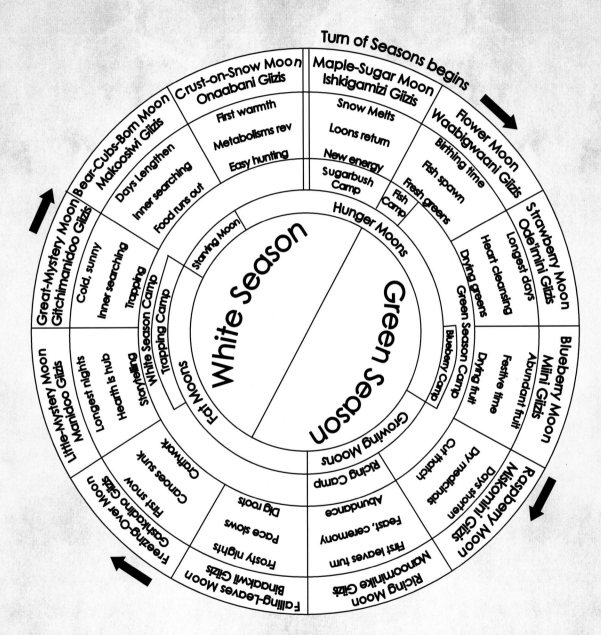

The circular diagram "Moons of the Northcountry Natives" is divided into two halves: **White Season** and **Green Season**.

Maple-Sugar Moon / Ishkigamizi Giizis — Snow Melts, Loons return, New energy, Sugarbush Camp, Fish Camp

Flower Moon / Waabigwaani Giizis — Birthing time, Fish spawn, Fresh greens

Strawberry Moon / Ode'imini Giizis — Longest days, Heart cleansing, Drying greens, Green Season Camp

Blueberry Moon / Miini Giizis — Abundant fruit, Festive time, Drying fruit, Blueberry Camp

Raspberry Moon / Miskomini Giizis — Days shorten, Dry medicine, Cut match, Riding Camp

Ricing Moon / Manoominike Giizis — First leaves turn, Feast, ceremony, Abundance, Growing Moons

Falling-Leaves Moon / Binaakwii Giizis — Frosty nights, Pace slows, Dig roots

Freezing-Over Moon / Gashkadino Giizis — First snow, Canoes sunk, Craftwork

Little-Mystery Moon / Manidoo Giizis — Longest nights, Hearth is hub, Storytelling, White Season Camp

Great-Mystery Moon / Gichimanidoo Giizis — Cold, sunny, Inner searching, Trapping, Trapping Camp

Bear-Cubs-Born Moon / Makoosiwi Giizis — Days Lengthen, Inner searching, Food runs out

Crust-on-Snow Moon / Onaabani Giizis — First warmth, Metabolisms rev, Easy hunting

Center: **White Season**, **Green Season**, Starving Moon, Hunger Moons, Fat Moons, Growing Moons

the *Hunger Moons*. The Fat Moons begin at the end of the Green Season and run into the heart of the White Season, while the Hunger Moons start at the end of the White Season and continue into mid-Green Season.

The Moons and Gender

Because Men generally have more kinetic energy than Women, and Women have more potential energy than Men, the Hunger Moons and Fat Moons affect each gender differently. Men are designed to move: they have higher muscle-to-body-mass ratios than Women, whereas Women are designed to nurture: they have higher fat-to-body-mass ratios than Men. Since Men burn more energy and have less energy reserve than Women, they are usually the first to feel the effects of the Hunger Moons.

Women, on the other hand, have an innate sustainability to carry them through the Hunger Moons. This is because of their need to continue nursing and support pregnancies. Even with these high nutritional demands, Women fare better than

Men because of their energy reserves and low personal energy needs. Additionally, Women conserve energy by ceasing Moontime bleeding.

This has a dual benefit:

○ Sufficient calories to support new pregnancies are not available during the Hunger Moons.

○ These pregnancies would result in births in the White Season—the most inopportune time, as the Child will be out of sync with the turn of the seasons. Food is scarce. The Child will end up in a cradleboard through the entire Green Season, and then start walking during the deep Snows of the White Season—a difficult time for a Toddler to get around.

Another factor affecting the total calories available to the People during the Hunger Moons is that Men, with minimal energy reserves, need to continually consume adequate amounts of meat and fat in order to continue the high-energy activities of hunting and trapping. Even when Women are as active

as Men, they need fewer calories than Men to fuel themselves.

Whether Fat Moon or Hunger Moon, whether Woman or Man, there is one constant: the People spend only a couple of hours a day on average (time varies from Moon to Moon) to meet their needs for food, clothing, and shelter. As you read on to explore what is done to meet those needs in each Moon, keep in mind that the majority of time is spent on the qualitative aspects of life—the social, cultural, and contemplative involvements that give life its warmth and meaning.

It is more accurate to state that *all* of the People's time is spent on these qualitative involvements. The People do not compartmentalize their activities, as we do, with distinct and separate times for work, shopping, socializing, and so on. In fact, most Native People have no word for *work*. Nearly everything they do is fun and fulfilling: meal preparation and berry gathering are social activities, hunting is a sacred event, and so on.

Moons and Months

If you are unfamiliar with Northwoods Native lifeway, it might be difficult for you to place the Moons in their appropriate seasons. Matching the Moons with their parallel calendar months would

seem to be a simple solution. However, it would be misleading because:

○ A moon is a bit shorter than a month, so each falls at a different time.

○ Moons are fluid. Since they reflect variables such as the weather, gathering and hunting, and the activities of the Relations, they can occur earlier or later than previously, or perhaps not at all. If the Blueberries do not bear fruit, there is no Blueberry Moon.

In the same way that you would know when months occurred during the year if you named them after events in your life (such as Vacation Month, Christmas Month, Going-Back-to-School Month, and so on), you would know when the Moons of the People took place once you became familiar with them.

Unlike our calendar year, with its always-the-same months, weeks, and days, and its ever-predictable events, the days and Moons of the Clanspeople are ever-changing from one turn of the seasons to the next. *Onaabani Giizis*, the Crust-on-the-Snow Moon, might be sunny and mild once, and the next time around it will be overcast and blustery. Instead of forming a crust, the heavy Snow piles deeper and deeper.

Is this a frustration for the Clanspeople? Not at all! For them, the only constant is change, and every change brings its gifts. In this case, the deep Snow would maroon large Animals, making them even easier to hunt than if the Snow were crusted. Snowshoes, which are destroyed by Snowcrust, could now be used to enable the Hunters to reach the Animals.

Even though the names of the Moons sometimes change, it matters little to the People, as their lives are very much rooted in the reality of the now. They care not whether it be Tuesday or Saturday, or whether the Moons fall on the same days every turn of the seasons (which they don't). Rather than looking at a calendar, the People hold activities and observances when Zhaawan and Giiwedin say it is time.

To the People, time is the rhythm of the seasons and the coming and passing of the generations. Most of the People do not know how old they are. They might not be able to recall how many days it has been since a recently occurred event, and they may not know how many days it will be until the next. If we were to compare this with how time plays out in our lives, it could give us a feel for how it is to live in Balance with the seasons and their Moons.

THE HUNGER MOONS

IT NEARS THE end of the deepest cold of the White Season. Stores of fat are running low, and Animals being brought in by the Hunters and trappers are lean from having burned all their body fat to keep warm and active throughout the White Season.

These lean Moons are essential to the health and strength of the People, both Human and otherwise. The weak either die or do not have the energy to reproduce, and the strong pass their genes on to a new generation. On the other hand, we modern People grow weaker with each succeeding generation because nearly everyone, regardless of fortitude, reproduces.

Along with health and strength, these Moons are vital to happiness. Without the physical, mental, and emotional stimulation that hunger brings, there would be no lust for life. The Clanspeople would have little motivation to draw together for common purpose. Whether it be abundance or scarcity, feasting or fasting, they do it together. This is the Circle Way—the way of the Clan, the way we all lived before we knew the plow and the town.

Crust-on-the-Snow Moon: Onaabani Giizis

As Zhaawan's warming breath grows stronger and her visits become more frequent, the People greet Onaabani Giizis, the Crust-on-the-Snow Moon. Daytime temperatures now regularly rise above freezing and they drop below freezing at night, which forms an ever-hardening crust on the Snow.

At first this makes for hard walking for Two-Leggeds and the larger Four-Leggeds because they break through the crust, which bruises their shins. As previously mentioned, the crust is also hard on snowshoes, which is why this Moon is also called *Bebook-waadaagame Giizis*, or Snowshoe-Breaking Moon.

However, as Onaabani Giizis progresses, the crust often becomes strong enough to support a person's weight without snowshoes. This is a magical time, as there is greater ease of movement than at any other time during the entire turn of the seasons. Brush, deadfalls, and rocks are mostly buried beneath the deep Snow, whose crust provides a smooth, uninterrupted surface that allows quick and easy travel virtually anywhere—through Woodlands, over Lakes, and across Bogs and boulder fields.

Onaabani Giizis is often the first of the Hunger Moons, as stores of fat and meat run out around this time. The People consider this a gift and welcome the hunger it brings. Without the fat-hunger cycle, they know they would soon become weak, miserable, and ungrateful, and the Gifting Way would become no more than a faded memory. They realize that to honor and embrace the hunger is to grow strong and happy.

Sometimes Onaabani Giizis gifts the People with a reprieve from their hunger: for a short time, the snowcrust is strong enough to support them, but not the bigger Four-Leggeds. Their sharp hooves cut through the crust and they find themselves up to their bellies in Snow, which considerably slows their movement. Contrast this with it being the easiest time for the Two-Leggeds to move around, and you have relatively easy hunting.

Yet the Hunters bring back only as much food as their Clan needs, as that is the way of hunting in Balance. However, this could mean killing more Four-Leggeds than usual. They are already well into their Hunger Moons, so their fat reserves are depleted. A Human cannot live on lean meat, and in an extreme White Season, when the Four-Leggeds are on the verge of starvation, even their flesh wastes away. It would provide very little energy, so it would be discarded, and just the heads, spinal cords, and organs would be eaten, as they would still be rich in fat and very nourishing. This would necessitate killing far more Four-Leggeds to feed the People than if the flesh was edible.

This above-average kill is actually the People's gift to the Four-Leggeds. They are suffering and many will likely die. Their Clan has grown too large for White Season food sources to sustain all of them.

During this Moon, the Crows return—the first solid sign from the Relations that the seasons are about to turn. In honor of Crow, some of the Clans call this *Aandego Giizis*, the Crow-Returning Moon. The sight and sound of the Crows, along with the warm Snow-softening breezes carrying the smell of new Life, beckon the People to spend more evenings at their outside Hearth. Being sheltered by a lean-to, the outside Hearth is quite comfortable in all weather and has been used for meals and craftwork throughout the White Season.

With their metabolisms beginning to quicken, the People are feeling the coming season change inside themselves as well. They grow restless, knowing it is nearly time for the Sugarbush Camp.

Maple-Sugar Moon: *Iskigamizige Giizis*

The warming air and strengthening Sun cause the People to shed their furs, which are packed away in airtight sacks with Bug-repelling herbs. Along with the Humans, the warmth tickles the Buds of the Maples, making them thirsty. Like nurslings, they suck hard to draw the sweet, nourishing sap up from the roots. The Buds swell quickly, signaling the arrival of new Life—the beginning of a new turn of the seasons.

The People, with their food stores and body fat depleted after the White Season, are also thirsty. They need an easy-to-get and easy-to-digest source of energy for the coming time of intense activity. Fortunately, the Elder Maples have extra sap to gift, which provides much needed calories, along with nourishing minerals and enzymes. This is clearly *Iskigamizige Giizis*, the Maple-Sugar Moon.

Most of the sap is drunk fresh. It is often left out to freeze at night, and the ice is skimmed off in the morning. This concentrates the nutrients, as only the Water in the sap freezes. Some is boiled down until nearly all the Water is driven off and it turns to sugar. In this state, it keeps indefinitely and is easy to transport. This is a busy time, as sap that is not consumed or boiled down soon goes sour.

Sugarbush Camp

The Clans have just moved from where they were nestled deep in the sheltering Pines for the White Season to the Sugarbush Camp. This could be a trek of many miles for the whole Clan, pulling loaded toboggans through deep, wet Snow. This is their transitional Camp between their White and Green Season Camps, and the nourishing sap will give them the energy for the long trek to the Green Season campsite.

This might also be called *Baubaukunaataa Giizis*, the Patches-of-Earth Moon. In open and sheltered areas the Snow has melted away and the first smells of moist ground and musty leaves since *Gashkadino Giizis*, the Freezing-Over

Moon, bring smiles and warm memories to the People.

These signs of the coming Green Season are accompanied by the return of *Maang* (Loon)—a welcome sight for the People. As soon as the ice is out, Maang returns to the Waters of the Northern Lakes to raise her mournful call, beckoning the Clan to come back from the deep Woods and keep her company in their lakeshore Green Season Camp. This Moon could thus be called *Maango Giizis*, the Loon-Returning Moon.

In time the flow of sap diminishes and it grows bitter. The Snow is freshly gone and Animal populations are at their lowest. Many

have died due to predation and other challenges of the White Season. Those who have survived are the strongest, swiftest and smartest—the ones intended to pass their traits on to the coming generations.

Predators such as Wolves, and a variety of scavengers, do well during this Moon. Snow and ice-encased carcasses become exposed, and any Animals weakened by the long White Season who still linger are easy prey. Wolves and other carnivores find it easy to feed their newborn, who are typically born in Iskigamizige Giizis.

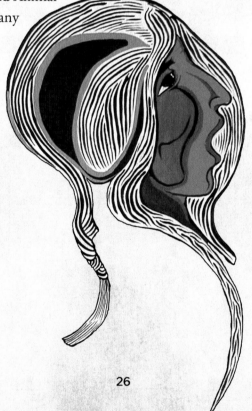

Flower Moon: Waabigwanii Giizis

This, the beginning of the Green Season, is the time of mating and birthing for most Plants and Animals. It is known as *Waabigwanii Giizis*, the Flower Moon. The term *Flower* is used metaphorically because the blooming is going on in so many ways. The warm breezes of Zhaawan pour northward; Rivers and Bogs, pregnant with meltwater, are bejeweled with returning Ducks, Herons, and Cranes; and Spring Peepers and other Frogs and Toads crowd the Woodland ponds. The incessant, screeching din they raise during their evening mating orgies could drive someone crazy who had to spend a night in their midst. Along with this blossoming Animal Life, we must not forget the explosion of plant blossoms.

Fish Camp

The warming Waters are telling the Fish it is time to mate. On their way to Green Season Camp, the Clan sets up a temporary Fish Camp on the shore of a good Walleye Lake, where at night they move onto their spawning beds in the shallows. Going out in their canoes, the Hunters illuminate the Fish by torchlight to spear them.

Suckers, a medium-sized bottom-feeding Fish, run in droves up the small streams to their spawning beds. At this time they are easy to catch, even by Children. Sometimes they can be scooped out of the shallows with little more effort than picking berries off of a bush. They can also be "tickled" in deeper Water by reaching down until one feels a Fish swimming over one's fingers and then gripping the Fish and flipping him up on shore. Nets, traps, and weirs work well also.

Together with Walleye, Northern Pike, and Musky, Suckers provide an abundant, easy-to-digest protein source—often the first fresh meat in Moons. Along with meat, the Fish gift the People with nourishing roe (eggs). Some of the females'

MOSES AMIK S.L.B. 03

bellies are so filled with them that they look ready to burst. It is no wonder that many of the Clans know this as *Namebini Giizis*, the Sucker Moon.

Along with the explosion of Animal matings and birthings, Woodland Flowers (many of whom are edible) push rapidly up through the carpet of leaves matted down by the Snow. They must take advantage of the small window of abundant sunshine on the Forest floor that makes it more resemble an open, Sun-drenched Prairie than the cool, deeply shaded setting it will soon be.

It is not only the succulent Plants of the Forest who are flowering, but the Trees themselves. Their Buds are swollen by the onrush of sap, and the Maple Flowers and Birch and Aspen catkins have burst forth, transforming the Forest canopy into clouds of silver, gray, and burgundy. It's easy to see why some of the Clans call this *Zaagibagaa Giizis*, the Budding-Leaves Moon.

The Clanspeople have subsisted on a heavy diet of toxin-producing meat and fat throughout the White Season, so they need a metabolic cleansing. They enact a Waabigwanii Giizis Cleansing Ritual, asking for help from members of the Heath family, particularly Blueberry, Labrador Tea, and Leatherleaf. These herbs are emetic, with their bitter principles stimulating blood and cell flushing. This cleansing is a major contribution to the Clanspeople's overall health.

Greens, being high in fiber, are an important part of the diet during the White Season because they scour the gut of accumulated plaque and parasites. Stores of dried greens are often depleted by this time, and meat and fat—a primary component of the White Season diet—have no cleansing ability because they have very little fiber.

Now filling the scouring role are fresh greens, blossoms, and catkins, which are in abundance. They are eminently digestible and best fresh, so rather than gathering them to take back to Camp, the Clanspeople follow the example of *Wawashkeshi* (Deer) and *Makwa* (Bear) and graze. When passing through the digestive system, this plant matter acts as a sponge, absorbing accumulated toxins.

The Plants are more than willing to gift themselves to the People, because they grow stronger with pruning and thinning.

Even with the continual hunger and focus on cleansing, this is a joyous time, as everyone knows it is preparation for the coming gifts and adventures of the Green Season. From a Life of connectedness to the means and ends of their existence, they are aware that hunger brings passion. Without hunger, Life would seem flat—there would be little reason to get up with the dawn, to learn a new skill, to seek healthy relationship. Without cleansing, their bodies would not be able to fully assimilate the cornucopia of nourishment the Mother is gifting them. They would be unable to fully partake of the many other gifts of the Green Season. And they would not be in condition to approach the White Season with relish.

Another flowering is the birth of Children, as Waabigwanii Giizis is typically when birthings occur. The weather has warmed, there are fresh greens to produce rich milk, and there is a hunger in the People's hearts for all of the new Life that Waabigwanii Giizis brings. Children born now, just as with the Plant and Animal Relations, have the entire Green Season to be nourished by the abundant gifts of Zhaawan and thus grow in strength and awareness to be well-prepared for the coming White Season.

The Babies born in the last Waabigwanii Giizis are now learning to walk, and there could be no better time to be outside and explore the newly opened landscape. Having been in the cradleboard through the White Season, they were easy to care for in the tight confines of a lodge.

Green Season Camp

Right after the Babies are born, the Clan moves to its Green Season Camp. An opening on the east shore of a Lake is chosen, where the westerly breezes coming off of the Waters will help keep the Camp cool and free of biting insects.

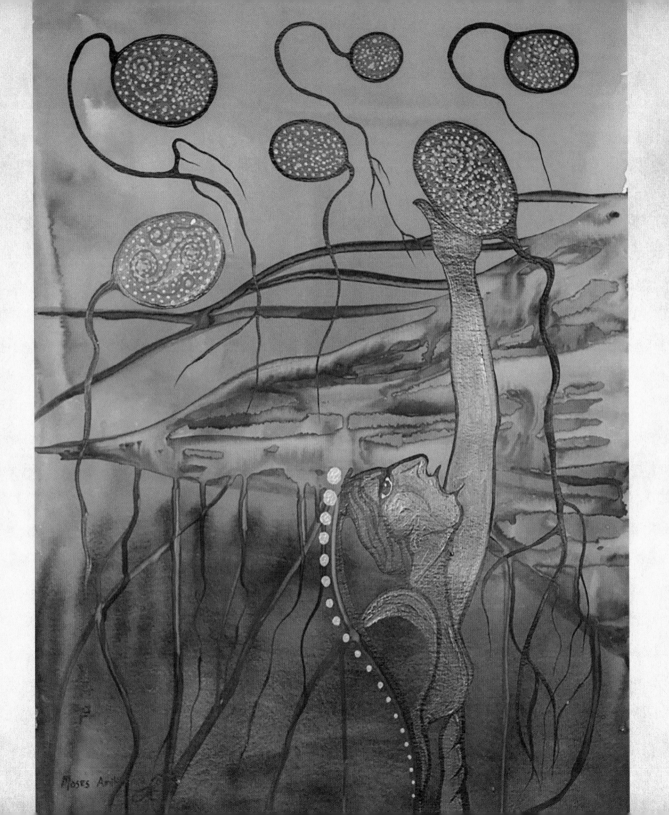

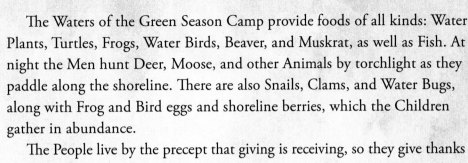

The Waters of the Green Season Camp provide foods of all kinds: Water Plants, Turtles, Frogs, Water Birds, Beaver, and Muskrat, as well as Fish. At night the Men hunt Deer, Moose, and other Animals by torchlight as they paddle along the shoreline. There are also Snails, Clams, and Water Bugs, along with Frog and Bird eggs and shoreline berries, which the Children gather in abundance.

The People live by the precept that giving is receiving, so they give thanks before, rather than after, they are gifted. Prior to anything being gathered or hunted, and prior to retrieving their submerged boats—even before Camp setup—they conduct a Ceremony honoring the Water, Earth Mother's blood.

The Keeper of the Waters Ceremony

Akin to the Dragon of the Far East, the Keeper of the Waters is a usually-be-nevolent underwater spirit-creature. She is held in such deep regard that her name is seldom uttered in public. In order to honor her and ask for protection when venturing forth on the Waters, each person gives an Offering of a piece of clothing, which is tied into a bundle and floated out to her.

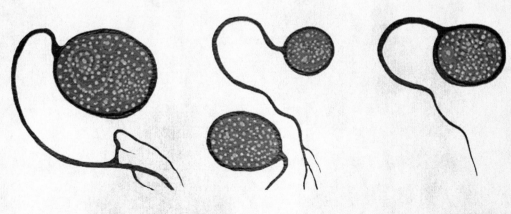

Waterways are the thoroughfares of the Northwoods. Travel by canoe is easier than overland, especially with heavy or bulky goods such as Animal carcasses or rolls of bark and root. With sister Clans also living on the Water, visiting and sharing news is greatly facilitated. Also, the open Waters make it easy to watch the comings and goings of various Peoples, related or unrelated.

With the days getting longer and the increased activity needed for moving Camp, along with the myriad of Green Season involvements, hunger plays the role of motivator. There's no choice but to move Camp, gather early greens, and catch Fish. Yet the Clanspeople do not see this as a matter of necessity. They are excited by the prospects of the coming season, and Zhaawan brings with her an extroverted, multidimensional energy that affects every living being. The Clanspeople feel a yearning to be involved and active, and they find themselves able to carry on several projects and activities simultaneously.

Hunger Persists

Even though there appears to be an abundance of food, the Clan is still in the midst of the Hunger Moons. Rather than being caused by a shortage of food, hunger is the result of a shortage of calories. Like the People, the Animals are lean. There is not yet any fruit, and starchy-rooted Plants have sent all their energy up into their stems to grow and reproduce.

Moses Anik 5.L.Bj 04

Strawberry Moon: Ode'imini Giizis

The Hunger Moons continue into the time of the ripening of the first fruit, which is *Ode'imin* or *Strawberry*. This is a time of great celebration for the Clans because, along with the physical cleansing that has been going on for the prior two Moons, there is now a cleansing of the heart. The literal translation of Ode'imin is *Heartberry*, because legend tells of Ode'imini being given to the People as a medicine berry to help heal the diseases of the heart. Thus, this Moon is known as *Ode'imini Giizis*, or literally, the Heartberry Moon.

Ode'imin was not given for the typical cardiovascular ailments we are familiar with, such as arteriosclerosis or irregular heartbeat, but for heart sicknesses such as jealousy, anger, and lying, and for imbalanced behavioral patterns that cause hardening of the heart.

You'll notice that the Strawberry is shaped like a heart. A principle of natural healing is that like heals like: if I have a weak liver, it would be helpful for me to eat liver; if I have weak bones, it would be good for me to eat bones. Healing the heart is healing more than just an organ that pumps blood; it is our center—the center of being.

When we speak from the heart, we are not just speaking from that blood pump; we are coming from the place where feelings, thoughts, intuition, the senses, and ancestral memories all come together in a talking circle to share their wisdom and craft the heartvoice. This greater heart is called the heart-of-hearts, and the voice of the heart-of-hearts is one's personal truth. When we speak from our heart-of-hearts, we speak our truth.

In this time, the Clanspeople give conscious energy to cleansing the heart-of-hearts. It, just like the body, accumulates toxins—psycho-emotional sludge from the intense introspective focus of the White Season. This sludge creates blockages that result in inefficient functioning of the heart-of-hearts. Hearing one's heart voice becomes difficult, causing reactiveness and inability to clearly express thoughts and feelings.

The ritual consuming of the Heartberry empowers this cleansing process, which is guided by dreams and by the Elders. Sometimes, thanks to Zhaawan's kinetic energy, contrary energies play a role.

It is easy to see why this Moon is called Ode'imini Giizis in honor of the Heartberry and the tremendous gift she brings to the People.

The Passionberry

Red is for passion, and the Heartberry is red, so some people confuse passion with assertiveness, competition, and even anger. Rather than passion, these behaviors are likely the acting out of dysfunctional patterns that were established in childhood as coping

mechanisms. They often persist in adulthood because they are reinforced by the dominant culture as positive behavioral characteristics.

The Heartberry is cool and sweet to the tongue, and this is the intended way of passion. It is the inability to stay in bed in the morning because of the allure of the unfolding day; it is thirst for nourishing relationship; it is the unyielding urge to be involved in what really matters in life; it is the lust to be fully immersed in the now—to be a fully alive, aware, and attuned Truthspeaker.

The longest days of the turn of the seasons are now. Zhaawan's explosive, nourishing energy is at her peak. Although the Hunger Moons still persist, the abundance of eggs and insects are providing more fat than the Clanspeople have seen in a long time. They are busy drying edible greens for their White Season, as this is the only Moon in which greens can be gathered in such abundance, and at this time they are at their most nourishing.

Blueberry Moon: Miini Giizis

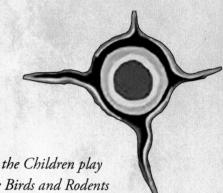

As the last of Ode'imin ripen, the first of *Miin* (Blueberries) take on a frosty blue tinge—the sign the Clanspeople have anxiously awaited. This is the most festive time of the Green Season, for this is *Miini-Giizis*, the Blueberry Moon. In the turn of the seasons it is second only to *Manoominike Giizis*, the Ricing Moon. A visitor only has to walk into Camp to pick up on the lively energy and joyful atmosphere.

Blueberry Camp

Most of the Elders, Women, and older Girls gather their berrying baskets and bedrolls and trek to the often Fire-maintained Meadows, which are carpeted from one end to the other with the low-growing berry. There, they choose a site on the sunny, windward side of a nearby hill, where Miin will dry quickly, to set up Blueberry Camp. Young Children come also, as they play a vital role in the harvest. Mats or sheets of bark are laid out in the Sun to dry the berries upon, and the Children play nearby to keep the Birds and Rodents from feasting.

This is one of the most important gathering times in the turn of the seasons, as Miin are easy to gather in quantity, they dry nicely, and they store well. With wide-tooth combs, the berries can be literally raked from the bushes.

Every night the drying berries must be poured into lidded rawhide and Birch bark containers to keep them from reabsorbing moisture during the damp nights. After they are dried enough that their sugar concentration can keep them from molding, they are stored for the White Season in airtight containers sealed with pitch.

Late Miin will keep ripening for two more Moons; however, as soon as the peak of the ripening is over, the berries are not as easily gathered or efficiently dried, so the Clanspeople pack up and return to Summer Camp.

Moses Amik SLBJ 03

THE GROWING MOONS

THIS IS A time of rapid growth for young Animals, as the weather is mild and lush greens, insects, and small prey Animals are abundant. An exception is late-born fawns, who quit growing early so they can reroute growth energy to putting on fat in order to be prepared for the coming White Season.

For adult Humans and other Animals, this is a transitional time of about two Moons to flesh out again after the Hunger Moons and catch up on energy reserves before putting on surplus fat for the White Season.

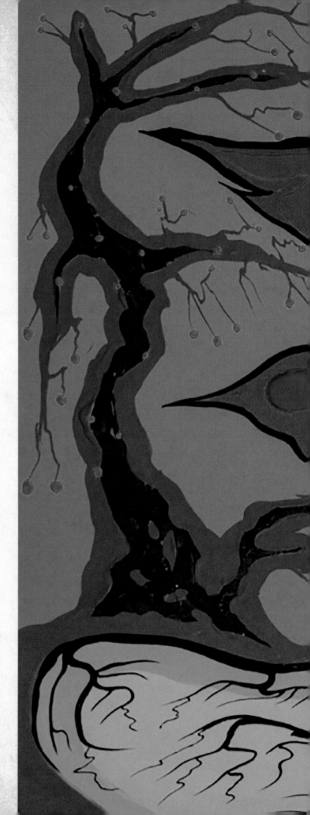

Raspberry Moon: Miskomini Giizis

Miskomin (Raspberries) are now in their prime and the Women and Children comb the Raspberry patches in the Forest clearings for the sweet, juicy treats. They are not as important a food source as Miin, because they are not quite as easy to gather, and they are more difficult to dry (they are often mashed and spread out on bark to make fruit leather), yet they are considered a delicacy, so they are enthusiastically gathered and prepared.

Although this is known as *Miskomini Giizis*, the Raspberry Moon, many other berries are gathered: Blackberries, Bunchberries, Gooseberries, Currants, Black Cherries, and more. Most of them are not as bountiful as Raspberries, yet they are harvested and appreciated for the culinary and nutritional variety they give to the diet.

As Miskomini Giizis progresses, the Elders note that days are getting noticeably shorter. This is the time to gather medicinal greens. Plants are sought out who had to struggle for their existence—the stunted ones growing in less than prime conditions—who thus became sinuous and resilient. Their labor made them potent in the essential oils and bitter principles that give them their medicinal properties. These medicinals are gathered with ceremonial respect, dried quickly in the shade, and stored in air-tight containers. If the season is dry, the medicinals might be left hanging from the ceilings of the lodges.

For some of the Clans this is also *Manashkoziwe Giizis*, the Gathering-Thatch Moon. As the days shorten and the nights get cooler, the first frosts tinge the Sedge Meadows, which toughen up the Grasses, preparing them to withstand the coming ice and Snow in protecting their roots and tender Buds. The Marsh and Meadow Sedges are ready to harvest when they begin to relax and lay down. At this time they show a bluish tint in the midday Sun.

Lodge-thatching Grass gathered now is tougher and more rot resistant than that from early in the Green Season, so it lasts several turns of the seasons longer.

The waning of Miskomini Giizis signals the end of the Hunger Moons. Animals are rapidly putting on fat; the Clanspeople, who feast on the Animals, are gaining fat as well.

Ricing Moon: Manoominike Giizis

While thatch is being cut and laid out in sunny areas to dry, the seed of another Grass that grows in the mucky shallows of quiet Waters is maturing. The People call it *Manoomin*, and we know it as Wild Rice. Although Manoomin is not a major part of the year-round diet, it is an important seasonal food, consumed in some quantity during the White Season. In honor of Manoomin, this Moon is called *Manoominike Giizis*, the Ricing Moon.

Each Lake has her own family of Manoomin, which is adapted to the unique conditions of that Lake: water temperature, acidity, fertility, growing medium, and wave action. For these reasons the Manoomin on different Lakes ripens at differing times, and each has differing years of abundance.

The Clans have Ricing Chiefs, who watch over the Manoomin on the various bodies of Water and keep track of its maturing. They determine if and when the Manoomin is ready to harvest on each body of Water.

Ricing Camp

Everyone awaits the Ricing Chief's announcement, as it signifies the time to move to Ricing Camp, which is set up on the shore of a Lake with a bountiful rice crop. Unlike Blueberry Camp, everybody goes to Ricing Camp, as it is the setting for the most important ceremonial time of the turn of the seasons.

This is a time of festivity and abundance. The Clans come together in force— it's their last opportunity to see each other before the Clans disperse for the White Season. Relationships are renewed, young people have the opportunity to meet each other, news and goods are exchanged, and there is much feasting. During this Moon of plenty, the lost weight of the Hunger Moons is regained, Women's Moontime bleeding returns,

and pregnancies are initiated. Babies, now several Moons old, have grown strong and are ready for the change of the seasons. There is much feasting—much to be thankful for. And this time when the Clans have gathered together is occasion for Ceremony: Naming, First Blood, First Hunt, Matedness, and Sweat Lodge Ceremonies, and, of course, the First Harvest Ceremony in honor of Manoomin.

Manoomin is the symbol of this sacred, celebratory, and transformative time. Because of this, it is a Sacred Food. The People have a Sacred Food to represent each of their four basic food groups, which are here listed and followed by their Sacred Food:

- **Meat and Fish**: Deer (*Waawaashkeshi*), Moose (*Mooz*), or Caribou (*Adik*) in the Far North

- **Berries**: Strawberry (Ode'imin), or Blueberry (Miin) where Ode'imin does not grow

- **Grains**: Wild Rice (Manoomin), the only grain in the Northcountry

- **Vegetables**: Fiddlehead Fern (*Waagaagin*), one of the first available Green Season greens

Waawaashkeshi mothers eat Waagaagin in abundance to produce rich milk for their newborn fawns. Hunters will eat Waagaagin as well so they smell like the surroundings and thus will not tip off Waawaashkeshi, who has an acute sense of smell, to their presence.

The sacredness of Manoomin is evident in the makeup of its name. Native languages are living languages, with each word telling its own story of place, purpose, and relationship. *Manoomin* is the marriage of two words: *manidoo*, which means *mystery*: more specifically, the great, unfathomable miracle of existence—the incomprehensible, the unexplainable; and *miinoom*, which means *something special* or *a delicacy*. Another possibility is that Manoomin is derived from *mino* (good) and *miin* (seed). The Elders refer to Manoomin as *Manidoo Gitigan*: from the Mystery's Garden. Truly, Manoomin is a Sacred Food.

In keeping with the festive atmosphere of this Moon, it might also be called *Waatebagaa Giizis*, which means Bright-Leaves Moon. The Maples along the shoreline are some of the first to turn, and they are the most colorful, showing off their bright oranges and crimsons against the green background of the deep Forest. They are the first hint of the coming season change.

Hazelnuts, Walnuts, Butternuts, and Acorns come to maturity at this time, and in good years they are gathered in great quantities and laid out to dry in the Sun, similar to the way Miin (Blueberries) are dried. As with Miin, the Children play around the drying nuts—and have the opportunity to improve their trapping and snaring techniques—to keep the opportunistic *Agongos* (Chipmunks) and *Ajidamoo* (Squirrels) from helping themselves.

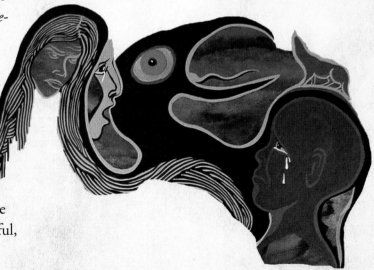

Moses Amik S.L.B 05

THE FAT MOONS

THE DAYS HAVE grown short and the nights, long. The pace of activity, though steady, is not nearly as intense, nor are activities as varied, as during the height of the Green Season. These are the *Fat Moons*: Plants and Animals are slowing down, as they are charged with stored energy from the growing season. The Clanspeople have an abundance of dried foods in storage, and roots and tubers are buried in nearby pits for easy access during the White Season. The Animals the Hunters and trappers bring in are layered with rich fat.

Women burn fewer calories than Men during the Fat Moons, so they generally put on proportionally more weight than the Men. This, along with the seasonal abundance, allows Women to rebegin their Moontime bleeding. Most pregnancies are initiated early in the Fat Moons—the ideal time because of available nutritional support and the fact that the Child will be born right at the onset of the Green Season.

Falling-Leaves Moon: Binaakwii Giizis

As Manoominike Giizis comes to a close and the activities of the Ricing Camp wind down, the first of the leaves are drifting down to newly carpet the Forest floor. This is the beginning of *Binaakwii Giizis*, the Falling-Leaves Moon. The Clanspeople take this as the first sign of the coming change of seasons, and they feel a nervous energy—an urge to move.

White Season Camp

At this time the Elders consult with the Minisino (Guardians) about locations they have come across during the previous season that might meet the criteria for a good White Season Camp: an inland location protected to the north and west from the biting breath of Giiwedin; a centralized location for White Season gathering, trapping, and hunting; and a location from which it will be relatively easy to move to the Sugarbush and Green Season Camps.

The White Season Camp is set up as quickly as possible, with all hands participating, because there will be a scramble to get all the hunting and digging of edible and medicinal roots completed, as well as their drying and storage, before freeze-up.

This is the beginning of a more introspective time for the Two-Leggeds, and for many of the Four-Leggeds. Like the Four-Leggeds, the Clanspeople go into a state of hibernation around this time. Theirs is not a deep sleep like that of the Plant People, Agongos, or Makwa, but rather a slowing down more like that of Beaver (*Amik*) and Waawaashkeshi. Like them, the Clanspeople's metabolisms slow down a bit in order to conserve energy. They stay closer to the Hearth than they might in the Green Season. They sleep longer and are more single of focus than in the Green Season. Where they might typically have had three or four things going at once, they are now more inclined to get involved in only one project and follow it through to completion.

53

During this introspective time, dreams, the deeper meaning of things, and the truth in another's words become ever clearer. The guidance of *Dodems* (Plant and Animal guides), Elders, and the Relations takes on new significance.

Freezing-Over Moon: Gashkadino Giizis

"When the first cold night forms a thin sheet of ice along the shoreline, and the morning breeze cracks it up, making it tinkle like breaking glass, it's the beginning of *Gashkadino Giizis* (the Freezing-Over Moon)," says Kamgaabwikwe, my honored Ojibwe Elder. When the Sun rises, the ice quickly melts away; yet it is a prelude to the coming days when the ice will not relinquish its grip. Rather, each night under cover of darkness it will creep farther and farther out on the Lake, until it has completely bridged the open Water.

In anticipation of the coming ice, canoes are weighted down with rocks and sunken deep, where they will be safe. The major preparations for the White Season are completed: snug moss-insulated lodges, a variety of securely stored foods, and a good supply of *ikwemitig* (Woman Wood). Sometimes called *Squaw Wood*, this is special thumb-diameter cured hardwood for the indoor Hearth. It gives a hot Fire, burns smokeless, and does not throw sparks. It is called ikwemitig in honor of the Women who gather it and tend the Hearth Fires.

Gashkadino Giizis appears to be a more relaxed Moon than those leading up to it. In many senses it is, as the intense activities around the harvest, along with the focused energy to set up White Season Camp, are now past. There is time to relax around the Hearth. Yet if one looks more closely, he notices that the Women, even though sitting and talking, are at the same time repairing furs and footwear for the coming White Season. Men are readying traps and snares, snowshoes, and toboggans. The first Snows could come at any time during Gashkadino Giizis, heralding the beginning of the White Season.

Little-Mystery Moon: Manidoo Giizisoons

As the Snow piles up, the Clanspeople enter *Manidoo Giizisoons*, the Little Mystery Moon. It is a cloudy, snowy Moon, with temperatures staying cold enough that the Snow does not melt, but not as cold as they will be in the Moons following. During Manidoo Giizisoons are the shortest days and longest nights of the year.

Now the People can hear with different ears than in the Green Season. Besides the energy of this season being more conducive to listening and introspection, everyone is drawn closer to the Hearth, closer to each other. They consider the Hearth to be the center of their Life, from which all their activities radiate. Besides a cooking Fire, the Hearth is warmth and light, and these two gifts grow increasingly important with the short, cloudy days and long, cold nights of Manidoo Giizisoons.

When the Hearth does not provide enough heat to keep the Clanspeople warm, as in this season, they each don a second skin, gifted by their fur-bearing Relations. When that proves insufficient, the Clan builds a lodge over themselves and the Hearth, which they see as a third skin. With all being under the same skin and sharing in the same warmth, a sense of closeness is engendered that is unique to the White Season.

Living in such close quarters and spending so much time together would not be possible in the Green Season, when individuals are drawn to spread out in every direction with a myriad of interests and involvements. Now, when the Elder beats the drum four times to signal the start of storytelling, voices readily hush in anticipation. These stories are special, told only during the time when Snow blankets the Mother-Bosom. Giiwedin has brought special ears for the Clanspeople so they can truly hear the stories, and he has given the deep sense of Clan relationship it takes for them to together manifest the teachings of the stories.

The cold encourages the Four-Legged Hunters to put on thick pelts of fur. At the same time, the deepening Snow provides shelter for their prey, so they must move around more and work harder to feed themselves. This tells the Men it is time to begin trapping in earnest.

Trapping Camp

Many of the Men, along with a number of the older Boys, and perhaps an interested Girl or two, will go far out in the bush where the Four-Leggeds are abundant and set up Trapping Camps. The trappers spread out, with two or three to a Camp, and run three or four trap lines that radiate out from the Camp and loop back. The pattern of their trails, with the Camp in the center, takes on the shape of a cloverleaf. The Camp itself is usually no more than a simple lean-to with a reflector Fire. The pelts and meat are cached high in a Tree, to keep them safe from scavengers.

Trapping goes on for one or two Moons, until enough furs have been gotten to clothe all the Clan, along with some extra for gifting.

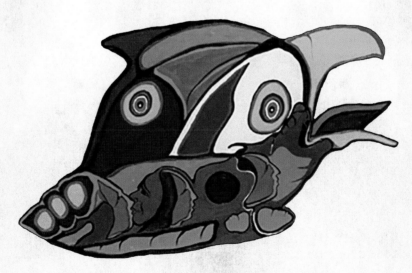

Great Mystery Moon: Gitchimanidoo Giizis

When Manidoo Giizisoons comes to an end, the skies clear, the Snow quits falling, and temperatures drop. As is the Gifting Way, the cold is balanced by clear, bright days, with afternoons feeling so warm in sheltered areas that, even though the air temperature is well below freezing, it is inviting enough to take tops off and bathe in nourishing, caressing rays of Sun Father.

This is *Gitchimanidoo Giizis*, the Great Mystery Moon—the height of the *manidoo*, or *introspective*, Moons. The exploration and unfolding of the mystery began in the last Moon, Manidoo Giizisoons, and it now continues in a grander sense and comes to a peak. This is when the greatest awarenesses of one's Life Journey are likely to come. Seasonal and personal energies are most supportive of exploring the big questions: Who am I? Why am I here? and What am I supposed to be doing with my Life?

Yet answers seldom come, because answers are dead ends. Rather, strides are made toward clarity. This process brings up more questions, and to question is to quest—to keep walking our Journey of Discovery. This is essential to living, for if we stood still, we would be merely existing. We would not be gaining in the understanding and wisdom needed to fulfill our reason for being by serving our People and the Relations.

In the process, fears and dreams, tears and laughter, come easily. In this Moon there is little distance between heart and mind, dreamtime and awake time. Story characters seem as real as the People in the next Camp, and it is as though the storyteller has just come back with news of their latest adventures.

The hunt goes on, only now in a manner that is more quiet, deliberate, and determined. The voice of the Animal is easy to hear, and the soul of the Hunter and the soul of the hunted can come so close that they know each other's needs and feelings.

In the pregnant (full) Moon of Gitchimanidoo Giizis, Dogwood (also known as Red Willow) is ritually gathered for the making of *Kinnikinick*, the sacred herbal mixture used for Petitions, Offerings, and Smudgings. Willow for basketmaking is also gathered, and some foraging is done as well, with Buds, catkins, and Woodgrubs giving welcome variety to the diet.

THE STARVING MOON

DEATH BY STARVATION is seldom a reality for Native People. Provided they are able to live their intended, unfettered lives, they can procure foods of nearly every type at nearly any time. However, if extreme hunger were ever to occur, due to extreme circumstances, it would likely be in the coming Moon. For example, if food stores ran short and there was no one to gather or hunt, or if disease or warfare debilitated the Clan, they would now be feeling it most. This is the last Moon of deep cold, when much fat, fur, and firewood is yet needed to sustain Life, and when stores can become depleted.

Bear-Cubs-Being-Born Moon: Makoosiwi Giizis

The deep cold continues into the next Moon, *Makoosiwi Giizis,* the Bear-Cubs-Being-Born Moon. Makwa is not a true hibernator. Even though her breathing and heartrate is considerably reduced, she can be awakened at any time. If there is a warm spell in the middle of the White Season—especially if she does not have enough fat to carry her through—she sometimes wakes up, comes out of her den, and wanders about.

When one of these warm spells rolls in during the night, the Clanspeople wake up to the Trees bejeweled with frost and a wispy fog drifting over the Snow. Their spirits are uplifted as they welcome the fog, which is the breath of the newborn Makwa cubs. It's the first sign of new Life and the coming turn of the seasons!

The People who are early to rise get to see the fog before the Sun burns it off. They joyously greet each other with, "Oh, Makwa is giving birth to her cubs!"

A thaw such as this (a common occurrence during Makoosiwi Giizis), along with the noticeably longer days and shorter nights, are the very first signs of Zhaawan edging her way northward to tussle with Giiwedin to bring on the Green Season.

The Human cubs are in their dens as well. Because of Women's Moon-times being in sync with the turns of the seasons, Babies born early in the Green Season are not yet walking, so they do not feel constricted by the close confines of the lodge, and they are easy to care for.

The foggy mornings of Makoosiwi Giizis remind the People that Onaabani Giizis, the Crust-on-the-Snow Moon, with its warm afternoons and easy hunting, is near. A new turn of the seasons is about to begin.

MOSES BEAVER SLB 00

AFTERWORD
THE SEASONS OF OUR LIVES

ANIMALS SPEAK TO Native People. The Wind whispers words of wisdom while lacing her way through the feathery fronds of the Elder Pines. Grandmother Moon guides the People through the recurring rhythms of the year. When I had a question about Life, my Elders would tell me, "Go and ask Owl," or "Watch the melting Snow." If I was depressed, they would remind me that the song of the returning Birds always comes to break the spell of a long White Season. When loss weighed heavy on me, the Elders spoke of how a season may go, yet it comes back around in its time. For Native People, everything is alive; everything speaks in a language that can be heard and understood.

Everything is a metaphor. That means everything is more than it seems—and other than it seems. My Ojibwe Elders told me stories of *Nanabozho*, the culture hero who has the ability to Shapeshift, i.e., to become something other than

he seems. Nanabozho most often Shapeshifts into a Rabbit, with the Shapeshift being a metaphor for what my Elders call *seeing the spirit side of things*.

You may have come to believe that the acumen to Shapeshift and see the spirit side of things is purely the privilege of shamans. If that were the case, we are then all shamans, as each of us has the innate ability to Shapeshift into anything. We only suffer from lack of practice. In time, Shapeshifting can occur spontaneously for us, just as it does for Native People, and we are able to see the physical and spirit side of things simultaneously.

When I asked Elders how I could restore my ability to Shapeshift, they would generally reply, "Be ever as a question, and listen deeply." I present their guidance on how to do so in my book *Truthspeaking: Ancestral Ways to Hear and Speak the Voice of the Heart* (Snow Wolf Publishing, 2019).

With deep listening, the turn of the seasons

Shapeshifts into the hoop of our lives. Each season becomes a metaphor for our periods of retreat, introspection, rebirth, and growth. The Hunger Moons, with the travails brought on by crusted Snow and the cravings for sweet succulence, provide a time for soul-searching and self-knowing. The Growing Moons that follow give the nurturance and support needed to integrate the gifts of the Hunger Moons. Then comes the Fat Moons—a time to listen to the stories from our Elders and the voices of our dreams. Yet clarity must be tested in order to become resolve, and that is the gift of the Starving Moon.

My fondest wish is that this story of the seasons, *Fat Moons and Hunger Moons*, becomes a guide for your Life. Read it as though you are reading about yourself. The story then becomes a mirror, a grounding, a window into your intrinsic being, and, perhaps, a guide to the next step on your Lifepath.

GLOSSARY OF OJIBWE LANGUAGE TERMS

Aandego—Crow-Returning

Adik—Caribou

Agongos—Chipmunk

Ajidamoo—Squirrel

Amik—Beaver

Baubaukunaataa—Patches-of-Earth

Bebookwaadaagame—Snowshoe-Breaking

Biboon—White Season

Binaakwii—Falling-Leaves

Dodem—Plant and Animal Guide

Gashkadino—Freezing-Over

Giiwedin—Keeper of the Northern Realm

Giizis—Moon

Gitchimanidoo—Great Mystery

Ikwemitig—Woman Wood or Squaw Wood

Iskigamizige—Maple-Sugar

Kinnikinick—A sacred herbal mixture used for ceremonial purposes

Maang—Loon

Maango—Loon-Returning

Makoosiwi—Bear-Cubs-Being-Born

Makwa—Bear

Manashkoziwe—Gathering-Thatch

Manidoo—Mystery

Manidoo Giizisoons—Little Mystery Moon

Manidoo Gitigan—From the Mystery's Garden

Manoomin—Wild Rice

Manoominike—Ricing

Miin—Seed

Miinoom—Something Special or a Delicacy

Minisino—Guardian

Mino—Good

Miskomin—Raspberry

Mooz—Moose

Namebini—Sucker

Nanabozho—The culture hero of the Ojibwe people

Nibinamik—Summer Beaver

Niibin—Green Season

Nokomis—Grandmother

Ode'imini—Strawberry or Heartberry

Onaabani—Crust-on-the-Snow

Waabigwanii—Flower

Waagaagin—Fiddlehead Fern

Waatebagaa—Bright-Leaves

Wawashkeshi—Deer

Windigo—The zombielike shell of a person who has been banished for a grave offense

Zaagibagaa—Budding-Leaves

Zhaawan—Keeper of the Southern Realm

INDEX

ACKNOWLEDGMENTS

WHILE THE WRITING of this book flowed as easily as Water down a mountain stream, the experience of the book involves much more than just my words. My cocreator, Moses (Amik) Beaver, had the intrinsic ability to capture the essential human experience on canvas, which brought my words to life. Our creative synergy was one reason we called each other "brother."

Moses's former wife Melanie Huddart contributed a number of the paintings in her possession, without which the book may not have been able to take form.

Dariya Quenneville and Ruth Goodman edited the text, and Brett Schwartz created the index. Serving as Ojibwe language consultant was my dear mate Lety Seibel. Sherry Roberts of The Roberts Group designed the book cover and interior, and Sherry's partner Tony Roberts crafted the e-book version.

Jenni Schulte, along with her mother Hildegard Schulte and friend Evelyn Koll, rendered the German edition. Elisabeth Demeter, Snow Wolf Publishing's German Division Managing Translator, oversaw the translation. Maria Sosa, in partnership with my mate Lety Seibel, created the Spanish edition. Alexandra Steussy-Williams, Managing Editor of Snow Wolf Publishing, was involved in each production phase of all three editions.

To everyone who helped birth this remembrance of a man whose kind heart and precious talent opened a door to a nearly lost world, I extend my deepest gratitude.

LIST OF ILLUSTRATIONS

Moses Amik · S.L.B

About the Authors

MOSES (AMIK) BEAVER was an Ojibwe artist from the isolated north-Ontario fly-in community of Nibinamik (Summer Beaver), which has a Nature-based culture that has remained largely unchanged from Civilized contact. His artwork depicts ancient teachings that remind us of our connection to each other and the natural world. He used his artwork to preserve the history, values, and spirituality of his people. In addition, he wished his work to become a way for everyone to understand the Aboriginal view of being "in and with the world, not masters of it."

Along with producing a rich legacy of paintings and wall murals, Moses was a traditional flute player and worked on Aboriginally themed stage productions. *Fat Moons and Hunger Moons*, Moses's second collaboration with Tamarack Song, was in progress when Moses passed on in 2017. Their first joint creation, *Whispers of the Ancients*, is a collection of twenty-three legends published by University of Michigan Press.

TAMARACK SONG is a writer, Native Lifeway instructor, and advocate of Nature-based healing who lives in a northern Wisconsin national forest. He is the founder of Snow Wolf Publishing and the Teaching Drum Outdoor School, and he is a cofounder of the Healing Nature Center. Authoring twenty books on living in Balance, he divides his time between writing and helping people renew their relationship with Nature.

Having grown up with forests and wetlands as his playground, Tamarack developed a strong relationship with Nature. As a child, he formed friendships with many wild Animals; and as a young adult, he lived for several years with a pack of Wolves. Though most people know him as a writer, his primary language is the one spoken by the Animals. His doctorate work is in developing ways to heal from the trauma caused by our fragmented relationship with Nature.

Made in the USA
Monee, IL
23 October 2021

80309497R00055